WHAT BOOKS PRESS

AN IMPRINT OF

THE GLASS TABLE

COLLECTIVE

LOS ANGELES

ONE STRANGE COUNTRY

STELLA HAYES

WHAT
BOOKS
PRESS

LOS ANGELES

Library of Congress Cataloging-in-Publication Data

Names: Hayes, Stella, author.
Title: One strange country / Stella Hayes.
Description: Los Angeles : What Books Press, [2020] | Summary: "In her debut poetry collection One Strange Country, Russian-American poet Stella Hayes replaces one strange country with another she calls home, mapping an origin story of identity, exile and loss.
-- Provided by publisher.
Identifiers: LCCN 2020026476 | ISBN 9780988924895 (paperback)
Subjects: LCGFT: Poetry.
Classification: LCC PS3608.A9435 O54 2020 | DDC 811/.6--dc23
LC record available at https://lccn.loc.gov/2020026476

Cover art: Gronk, *untitled*, 2020
Book design by Ash Good, www.ashgood.design

What Books Press
363 South Topanga Canyon Boulevard
Topanga, CA 90290

WHATBOOKSPRESS.COM

ONE STRANGE COUNTRY

For Dade, Margot & Finley

& for my mother Bella

& for Alla

CONTENTS

remember:
before battle we would do each other's makeup, comb each other's
        hair out
saying we are unconquerable, we are terrible and splendid —

        —*Dedication*, Franz Wright

How confused the bat must be: to come from a womb, yet be
called upon to fly. As if in flight from itself, it zigzags through the
air like a crack through a cup. In the same way its wing, at dusk,
crazes the porcelain surface of the sky.

        —*Duino Elegies*, Rilke, translated from the German by William H. Gass

OUT OF THE FRAME

She turns away out of the frame, slipping
out of a rough seam, folding laundry into canopies
blotting out first me, then her own hologram

which keeps splitting & splintering off.
She's shifted, she's brushing the grime
off her white teeth. She doesn't floss.

What's the use now that the shadows
are too wide. As postwar boulevards
releasing light into tunnels. Go quickly.

MONOLITH

I am in a memory, in the generation I lived among you.
I stand against a world that has no use for paper. The printing
press has outlived its usefulness. I am allowed to read the dictionary,
in a language I don't have any use for. One lacking a cover,

left in a recycling bin in a suburban alley. I look up words
that don't begin. They are suffixless. Our feudalism has evolved,
to an empire. Those who dissent are made to unlearn the alphabet by heart.
Not seeing you & you & you is like not having any more paper

resting, on the desk. The lines, color in the lines. Child plus child
& a dog to love. A hole to fall into, a hole to fall through
again & again. Will you have children? Will they be like you,
like no one could possibly be again? —

Speaking in soft voices to my apparition. I promise to make my
visits short. I transcend self-interest even here where a bell undergoes
a metamorphosis. Where stone equals stone. I don't want to know.
Please, someone. Anyone give me paper, so I can see through your face.

THE FLOW OF GOOD & EVIL

He used *struggle*, a word oversized for a boy. It lands
in his chest. On the surface are his broken small
invisible, to both of us, muscles that cause sharp
blows to his heart chamber.

We would both use struggle to describe an action. Like
the ski boot we couldn't buckle, the sand that wouldn't
stick to sand, the water that wouldn't flow from glass
to mouth. These were small. Struggle is oversized

for a boy whose calendar is dominated by small
events. Addition & subtraction. The lessons in good
& evil, in his daily workbook, are simple enough.
Don't stick out in the crowd. Tell. Don't tattle.

Listen to the unspoken. The simple allegories found
& lost. As the sun rests between his fingers. As it finds
itself, on the ledge of a large open elementary school
window. His eyes are fixed on his teacher,

who helped him find himself in 3rd grade. All beauty
is fixed; it is fixed on some object. That follows some
of the rules of nature. Let be end seem. When I got
lost on the beach one summer, I got to a bungee cord

that stretched to the ocean. Almost touching the nadir, that
halted my flow. I didn't want to find my way back to them.
The sand stuck en masse to my ankles. The flow of what
I had to unlearn & undo. The struggle of one among many.

SUNDAY MORNING

On this winter morning
black birds do not lullaby with a song
they do not fly south to sever

their wings from a black world
their cooling bodies recoiling
in flight like dying angels

on this morning
we are attuned to the deaf rustle
of the outstretched sheet

the bed a box
pillows two shapely squares
the mattress releasing its coil like a lung

it's not a difficult morning
the room is not cold
the walls are not hospital white

the toast coated in butter and jam
offers nutrition
the smell of coffee just bloomed

lapping up the porcelain cup
there's no talk of theology
no game of chess set

no commitment made to a morning service
the two children at breakfast
eating French toast sunk in butter and syrup

it is not a difficult morning
the soul stands up to being made extinct
it's not a difficult morning

it's not without hope
the newspaper turned to a particular page
it's not a difficult morning

it's not without hope the coffee pot
turned off the pan cooling
the kitchen halted to a stop.

FROM LA WITH LOVE

You fail to represent meaning
To your meaning-addicted daughter

Which curdles on the tongue
Thinning out like a blood clot

With whose meaning did you
Cross the ocean from LA

To small NY pulling
An immigrant's suitcase

And settled into kitchen sink
Discourse like Plato's

Forms your artillery of meds
Assert an oldness you'll pass

On to me my being
Is your being

You have beautiful
Lips that withhold beauty

You should never ask me
How things are not

Without small talk first that
I will peel off like a pill

From foil that lay
Dying in your hand

PORTRAIT OF BELLA

You folded up your grief
In the relief of your hands like a linen

Handkerchief embroidered with your
Mother's initials I believe your hands reveal

And conceal the musculature of your journey
To now in your daughter's makeshift

Painter's studio in NYC your aura illuminated
To your discomfort she paints without artifice

Her small knife cutting in the parts
Of you she believes conceal your frame

Is slightly smaller than when you arrived
At forty-three with a radiance of someone

Who left someone she loved for many
Years you and your daughters complete

A familial pieta as we fold stony
Into stone to the monument of grief

You've built from ground up as you behold
It and make more beautiful for all of us

AT THE BLUE PLATE IN SANTA MONICA

I fell through the night this time
Without you on the other side of me

The last day in a perennial breakfast spot
Nourishing writers on cool ocean-infused

Mornings your skin freckled but always pale
Blue underneath the sun doesn't stop its heated up

Rays the beams of possibly hope
The last day for the sun worshippers

And you with me riding out the underside
Of the sun ray that fell through the night

THE KNOWLEDGE OF WATER

I draw a bath
 and   wait
for the porcelain
to be made warm   enough
   for me

                         to step

                                    down
February   continues
   to   be

                              unbearable
                    pressing
on me with
  a supernatural force

                         my body
keeps betraying   me

                    a boulder for a brain   resting in a skull

my bruises   in   weightless

                                          conversation
with   the water

                 fall in

                                    and

resurface   like firewood

with you   again
under water
without
a face

the brain
a boulder
I'm filling up with you again

                        with almost no airflow

the silence
settles
  on my skin
                as I lift
myself out

BEACH-BOUND

Remember how we would look into each other
On the surface and beneath the skin
And just know the temperature of the hand
The gesture closing the stillness

Of the other parts of the body
Riding out the dynamism
Of two bound energies
How small we must look from above

A woman twined to an archetypal man
In the sun keeping warm the beachfront in front
The sand on the skin folding
If I stay on this beach long enough

I might forget the storm that keeps me unsettled
The tumults of the past broken up on the sand
In front of me demanding to be sorted and perhaps
Assembled into a new collage mostly

From sand the new palms stand on their elegant tall
Stalks and speak to me in murmurs
And whispers like my mother used to you are true she
Would utter when I would be lulled

Unaware that she was singing with a weakened voice a folk
Song learned for a college course taken out of a box for me
For the sake of language memory sounds of innocence
Brought to us here always taking us enslaved

And liberated from a closed womb to an emergent repassing
Of a familial line passing the little root, a rootling breaking
Through layers of dense rock and concrete
A blossom enclosed in itself a whisper

LET'S SINK

In a sandcastle at a seaside
Town with falling-in walls
Lusterfull sand hotter
On his skin than mine

Fixed together inside
A memorized memory of two
Bodies set in the
Mind's motionless motion

Sinking inside the fold
Of a mirroring dermis
Is this a lucky plate
I pick up from a sink

Maybe it's a very lucky plate
On its surface
Meeting an equally lucky fork
A window looking out

To a car on a driveway
Holding on
To March's snow
Too heavy to be lifted up

BIRTH'S ORDER

You
came   into   being
        in an instant

open   & alone
fluttering
        into my open arms

a girl with   almond-shaped eyes
 arriving fluent in arts
     music & ancient parable
  having learned it
    from a shade on
    the   inside

you decide to   discard the knowledge
of the womb
            for   the spirit
a moth returning to the mouth
     I
            am   dividing

  Let me chant
   my planned liturgies
accept me into
your sphere of spheres
   I like sitting with you
  chin against chin
            in   love

the wind making a circle for us   moving us in

to settle   into life

                            falling through

 from your   origin

 one by one
in birth's
 order
in death's order
 unnoticed in the curve
 of the fall

IN THE FISH TANK

We brought a fish tank home, for the fish
whose life you maintained in a non-gleaming,
modest fish tank. Replete with an underworld

of stiff plastic furniture, almost like someone's
home. You insisted, with the insistence of a juvenile,
that we introduce a friend to the boy fish

living alone in a fish tank in your room. So we did, undoing
the stiff plastic home of a happy fish. He, having tested many
a time, the fish tank's walls, and butting time and again

against the chaos and order of an underwater world
of a fish. We put him in a small holding vessel,
a plastic cup filled with tap water.

The fish's forebrain, put to a real and palpable
stress, was hard to watch. We brought in a new fish
tank, designed for a pair. The clerk at the pet store

held that this was the right fish tank. It came with a divider
wall, porous for water to wash through the contents, stiff
enough to keep the two fish always and forever apart.

TO THE LIVING, LIVING

I am hot in the lymphs. The soldiers
who dutifully fight off invaders

Those defenders of good against evil.
The upkeep keeps rising against the suns & moons

Descending on surfaces. A raised toilet lid,
Slicked in morning coffee,

Sliding down the esophagus like a single sun ray.
The cup contains the spill of the day

Against the good & evils
Spinning in the overheated lymphs

The beetle ascending the wall
Slides up & down as if on a surface of ice, leaving

An invisible trail of restlessness & despair,
I am helpless, as it is —

The other bugs in the hallway reform into moths,
Larvae in repose, gather around the source of the artificial light

That serves as a night lamp. Each morning
As in this one, we wake up to a massacre.

The organisms with long detached-like antennae,
Didn't make it through the shared night.

Their lives are as long as our night.
Is that why they huddle

Near the light, warming up to enlightenment?
At least they reached the light & died by morning

HAPPILY

If you wait for me
The oak tree will
Make a crown
Chockfull of crystals

If you wait for me
I'll donate my eyes
To endless
Scientific experiments
When I die

If you wait for me
I'll leave myself
Out in the rain to shrink

If you wait for me
I won't tell anyone
That you've waited

If you wait for me
I'll live in the clouds
For the both of us
Holding on to your hand
Letting up for air
Now and again

I'll keep floating through the
Supernatural funk
And wait for you
As you wait for me

ODE TO STRUNK AND WHITE

More rules than not embed the house
Washed in end of summer set off
From the dirt road in separation

Of water from dirt the spider languishing
On the piano key seems literate
The mouse loitering in the dust

Looks like a boy
The ghosts haven't yet decided
To stay on with the living

The field of tall grass in front
Of the Brooklin, Maine house
Stands at a right angle rules

And reminders of how to become
Delineated are a road map
Andy White warns in Section V

Against foreign languages
Ceci n'est pas une pipe
Doesn't make the cut

The Russian Futurists's Khlebnikov's
Specifically prefix suffix
Root play I sneak in other examples

Of usage and style ensure
This urinal is a fountain
Give me more readymades

To gobble up into being clear
None of us is perfect
The walrus and the carpenter

Were walking close at hand
Who knocks no one answers
None are so fallible imagine being

Left behind what is wanted is a few
More pairs of hands the linking verb will
Agree with the number of its subject

Throwing the reader a rope
To annex meaning to the root
The dash in rule No. 8 as only it can

With economy sets off the independent
Clause taking fall in the forest as a tree
One day will fall does not repay

I am drained of vigor I returned
and saw under the sun how a story
is strange fists bloody from the fight

The heroine maintains the punch
Until the tree falls in the pine forest
And the bantam rooster fans out its tail

And then there's *meaningful*
A bankrupt adjective Strunk is clear
On this and instructs the writer to choose

Another or rephrase I can't possibly
Replace it the well is bankrupt
And the water in it is stillborn

And the faces of the fallen-in
Coins washed away a picture hung
A man was found hanged by the neck

In the hallway a man hanged himself
Of his own free will in the hallway
I told a friend he hanged himself

My friend said you mean
He hung himself no that's not
How you say it you have to get it right

II

WALKING THROUGH THE UNDERWORLD

out my window colored heads bound in swiftness. in their decision to bring about movement
& motion. the snow is taking a break from falling, as it did just days before. the village is
painted in primordial gray, with roofs in color too happy even for a rainbow. eavesdropping
on a father being mourned at the mouth of the coroner's bed. the aroma of death. a father
& daughter lost to loss's gravity. a walk through the underworld would have to wait. his body
wasn't friendly overnight. forgetting that it was capable of carriage, despite the force of gravity;
forgetting it was self-possessed, despite being broken down. anyone it keeps bumping into
when awake; it made what sounded like a voice of pleasure. but as closely as I allowed myself
to hear the bedtime fury, he was letting out what sounded like a body's pain; wrestling to bring
itself respite. at least overnight. at least it should have been given a break. like in a fist fight
for survival. the mercury line inside the thermometer rising & rising. in cold flurries, the snow's
motion resting, motionless. he inside the fury. I am with him, right hand on his forehead; as he is,
inside a breath, cataloging heat & cold. in hope of cooling. in hope of slipping free from the heat.
I am crossing a field with banks of too much snow. the grieving child watching with her eyes,
as she has seen too much too. you won't recognize me. I see a twin likeness in the shadows,
under a thin light. we will be shadowless; skipping through somewhere where we can't
or won't want to be from

DAY'S BREAK

The day rose — again. Layers of the sun becoming instantly extinct.
The white sheet that overnight divided me from you.

The map resetting the brain, one syllabled synapse at a time.
Forming & reshaping a carbon footprint & possibly carbon making up

The pieces of infinity. As some scientists claim, we return
To carbon, in red schoolgirl ribbons.

If I snap, it should bend apart. Infinity plus the gift of today.
You stepped as far as the lip of the Golden Gate bridge. Ocean-salt

Accumulating, on breaking skin. As it almost swayed,
Like a dog's tongue, lapping up the end of a day. You pleaded for us,

To make our way back. To our day in San Francisco broken in half,
New York City left behind. An exile's life is planned one day at a time

With its lows & highs. We would turn back, in one column.
Slowly catching up with shadows. Already watchful.

Jumping off points of too many. You tell me on our drive up north,
The jumpers are lead. It spooks you. There is no turning back.

A sun, at a jumping off point, peaking at noon, yielding to a moon.
Resting in exile —

INDETERMINATE

It takes itself away toward
an indeterminate future
away & toward

   the ant

& its weightless imagination
spending its waning energy
on forgetting

      blanks on blanks   stopping

I see you building
    a cathedral

   Why do it
      this useless thing

almost   a body
        on legs
        almost   like yours

Almost like you're
building a new species
more ant
than human

not too heroic
with diminished expectations
more human
than ant

I mason a stone wall around our cathedral
to keep you   out
stone to stone as silent as   ruins
assisted by an unarmed army
climbing up strands   erased love
counting down days   months   years
compressing years   to seconds

AFTER THE RAIN

The morning opens up with a number
Of regular birds exchanging monologues.

To my untrained ear the tweets and chirps
Sound like the end of a healthy argument.

The morning forced me to look
At the tree branch obscuring your face,

And witness the raindrop yet to fall
Into your open hand across the many

Miles of ocean. I can see you,
Lifting the rain with your open

Hand. Like a rock in free fall.
And keeping it in that unnatural

Refrain, for what I mark as indefinite.
Would you share the rain with me?

AN EUCLIDEAN ORDER

In each star, a generation
Lay unawake, holding down
To atoms still unborn.

The tireless planets, held
Close in the embrace. Of that
Which is. All matter lay, undying

Swirling, in reticent rings
In repudiation of now.
Recasting the earth flat once again.

AMOUR ABSOLU

In a room
A crowd of well-wishers
Condolence utterers
Devour coffee and morning cakes

February's morning yawn
Enters the room
Unannounced sideways through
Stained glass

They offer rehearsed thin
Smiles and the thinnest
Cooling handshakes
And nothing is warm

You are held in a white shroud
A plain pine box
And nothing is warm
The well-wishers

Open and close their mouths
Like umbrellas
Devouring coffee
And cakes

It's the break from first love
That closes the heart
And like a first death
It makes no announcement

Like wings of a butterfly pinned
To a page in a notebook
I unpin my first love
Like my first death

I knew it once
My own slice of the sun
Ablaze with your love
In the shadow of the sun

IN THE FOOTSTEPS OF TELEMACHUS

They were in line in front of me in the food
hall underground not closed off from the
world in town for an annual theater catch
up trip NY was about to hand them a
standardized pleasure the lobster roll that
made it uptown

I was a NY veteran by now I took my hits
when & where I could today they drew me
in the food hall underground at the Plaza
Hotel below the pedestrian line between
58th and 57th Streets schlepped by carriage-
drawn horses and tourists in blindfolds

the single-screen pocket-small Paris theater
on 58th across from my underground
screening films for the people walking on
firm ground not for me years ago I saw
there the revival of *Belle du Jour*
with Catherine Deneuve playing modern

day Madame Bovary the femmes fatale are
home in the suburbs with their husbands &
kids going to bed with the disillusioned
moon I am thinking back to *Notes from
Underground* I read in high school for the
first time in translation in a small American

suburb clack click the shoes of pedestrians
fall on the man in the apartment
underground in the practice of misreading
footsteps up by escalator I emerge into the
held-captive trunk of Central Park met
by air made by hard-working public trees

the bums long-driven out to 5th Avenue
form into marble fragments as if on loan
from the antiquities room at the Met the 19th
century *A La Vieille Russie* parked
on 5th Avenue displays Carl Fabergé eggs
in the rectangular window begotten from

the Bolsheviks funding the cause of the
proletariat sold to Americans who like the
varnish of fallen aristocracies today caught
on camera by a domestic tourist
Tom is a soft-spoken novelist his diction
dispossessed of a once NY accent

Kathy was born in Brooklyn she's in sandals
& flowing skirt the three of us sit down
to eat together in one of the back sunless
rooms of the underground dining hall
the floors made of marble imported
from the Roman coliseum

in concealment of heartprints whose beliefs
rested face down on a coin tossed
into a fountain by a boy returning home
Tom isn't eating he's writing
as a professional writer Tom can't help
but read in me what is not transparent

a character detail that will be defining
he wonders what type of narrator
I would make in a story Tom asks me
for a dessert pick I point to the cake
boutique whose twenty-layered crepe cakes
make landfall on the palate

like Salome's skirts the boy who can be
Telemachus hair strung in hard large shells
runs ahead of me in his newly made steps
smaller than mine in the sand new steps
I walk & walk unable to catch up
to his new dazzling life just a few steps

up from mine a boy's life falls in the
distance a father hears his son's footsteps
fall as a grown man's for the first time
in twenty years his inward wound closes
footsteps heard in the distance
making footfall

THE LONG DRIVE

She packed up the portrait in the trunk
Of the updated station wagon. Face down, smoothing out the canvas,

Tucking in the four corners over underpinnings
Of the last of the summer garden which held —

Garlic stamen and stem, darkening green kale,
Wine-dark beets, bright-orange carrots, chamomile flowers that would,

Dry over fall & winter.
Potatoes holding on to dirt. Picked by gentle hands the night before

The failed morning hung on beside his dog,
In the back seat. She was so still, that I kept turning to see

If she were breathing —
My sister worked from a color photograph of him as a teenage boy,

From a garage-turned-studio, awash with northern cool light,
The portrait takes up what's left of her life. She keeps turning,

Upside down. She is Dorothy, caught spinning out & in.
Sometimes turning the house upside down.

The roots of the single apple tree, in the large backyard
Set against an old forest

We are driving away from the predawn lobster fishermen's
Morning pilgrimage. Out to the ocean that would pierce her shallow

Sleep & mine. The front bedrooms, facing
A desirable ocean front view. I toss my dream out the window —

Of the updated station wagon, as we make our long drive
Back home. Of walking on soft ground. Not this patch of ocean-

Deteriorated mix of weed-grass, across from a backcountry church
& a mechanic's garage that makes him a home. I don't tell her not to look back

As I should. I tell her to keep her eyes on the road —
Our drive will be long

We pull up to the apartment. She gets out first, the dog,
Then me. She picks up the weeklong portrait, winding it into a narrow

Roll, which for the duration of the drive, lay among a mix of household
Items, things that wouldn't make it through the corrosion of winter

Oceanside. The paints & brushes of an artist, things being hauled
Back to a big city life, root vegetables, contained in cloth bags,

That have taken root, without her permission

TOGETHER, ALONE

He asked for my help for a 4th-grade school project,
very late in the year. Too close to summer break,
somewhere skipping pebbles across

a surface of water. Help me find big, bouncy words,
suitable for poetry. One, in particular, happy.
Siri spoke pitfalls from unverified sources.

We were hit with joy, a safe synonym. A word,
I feel when I am with him. As I teach my son,
how to write a poem for a class assignment,

I turn to the transparency of one. *The Anecdote
of the Jar*. Alone, in the wilderness of Tennessee,
not solving our puzzle to write a suitable

poem. What about safety pins?
Which hold the air, one pin at a time, festooned
in miles of aluminum. He gave up on me,

as I offered inferior words. As did I, at least
for the night. Poetry would have to wait.
Not long before he fell asleep,

as I uncoupled a morning from a night.
He had what seemed like a very bad
dream. Eyes running wild behind closed

lids. He rose up in protest. Denying
the poem. Repeating over & over in his
sleep, certainly unaware that I was listening.

STRUGGLE

and   Roses sit   atop a bedroom

 Dresser

     aglow

      creeping up toward

My foreign sky

     Carve out just the right tone

         From that word that drips

From the tongue like the

           undecaying

      contour of you

     Surgically extracted and   possessed

    What could le mot juste be for this day

and this time   I think it's in the image

      The bowl of raspberries beckoning to be

   put in the mouth — one by one   And

      evaluated

TAKING DOWN THE NEW YEAR'S TREE

We started to take it down, in complacent gestures
of a husband & wife. Putting ornaments away with deliberateness,

into an assortment of aging boxes, of varying sizes.
It lurked in the dark. In ornamental exile.

With an unchaste smile, just moments before, having a point of view.
Now dressed down, in picked-over ornaments. It had a will to live

out its days. Without a root system to count on as it once had in the near-
by forest. We were diligent, adding water daily to a dish under its cut off torso.

To keep the luster of its needles shimmering. The arms,
strong enough for the ornamental weights, we hung to mark it as ours. For the days,

it stayed with us. Each day, caught off guard. In its fluorescent glow.
It wasn't stiff like a corpse — but it wasn't alive like

a tree having once lived. You know when something is living —
composed of blood, not chlorophyll.

It sinks life into you & you know it. You just do —
We unplugged the lights. And there it stood, in the nude, waiting for morning.

ONCE

I am awarded an ordinary happiness.
The one, inalienable.
    The one we're born with.

    The one in which the insane
are jacketed
    when they first arrive.

    In the curated
houses for the insane. I crave
    the ordinary —

    type of happiness.
The one that is removed.
    From you, when

    you move, from
child to adult.
    The one that doesn't grow,

    on trees. The one,
that's not free.
    The one that you would

    commit crimes for. Against those
you love. The one you wish —
    your heart would stop for.

DON'T TELL THE WOMEN

Small, we have the sun to unseat, holding it down, unrequited.
In the disfigured street, I left him. Our sun, unrequited.

The rooster stares into the sun, we are together for a day.
Read with me *Unreadable*, a fugue we make — unrequited.

I am lost to distance, quietly weaving a carpet.
Loom with me a fugue made of love threads, unrequited.

Don't tell the women, the moon & sun will be hushed.
Put into place, for an uncertain life, unrequited.

You saw drags of being in me to live up to, the sun to unseat.
Will you get water with me on our way up, unrequited?

Which tree will I inhabit, only the unrequited will know & tell.
I weave golden thread into the sun, rising to meet the day, unrequited.

When I discovered nihilism, I held on for more light.
The good it did — the sound of the moon, unrequited.

The pockets are overflowing with knowledge, replacing the sun.
I make up ruins, humming — unrequited.

If history is on repeat, I will be taken — again, left to hold on to air.
No, your father's star, you will not be held — by the unrequited.

I keep measuring out my life in breaths — holding on.
Let's do it, run away with one star for a map, unrequited.

UNTITLED II (IF I WERE A BIRD)

I would hope
You would build me a nest
From twigs and leaves

If I were hatched the day
The forest regurgitated its sap
I would ask for you to kick me

Out but I'm not a bird
With a collapsible skeleton
I don't live in a nest why pretend

That it would work living in a tree
And living off its sap we evolved
Into non-birds

The brain more capacious
Arms crossing the air
Useless as wings

If I could I would take flight
Into an aerial battle with gods
As warriors remaking things

A LOVE SONG

one more night to dismantle   like a toy
        train
      another day to be folded up and put in a
drawer
                 a continent to put out of sight
       another moon to unfill
one more vowel to blot out
      from the page
   another consonant to render useless
another veil to put over the eyes

         a flurry of word-colonies
          buzzing like fruit flies
in the ear

the tear duct at the ready
the iris filling up

      scenes of you play out

I long to close my eyes
         know that you are not in the dark

        that   I am
     that I have my hand in yours
     that you have not rubbed me
out with the pink eraser on the back of your   pencil

on   the page my sentences formed
 more of vowels than consonants
                                        hammer at the   closed scabs
formed along the way from child to adult
on   closer look
   they reveal what made them
the removal of childhood
                         from genesis in one strange country
to the placement in another whose
language is uninflected and dominated by
consonants

my eyes are still closed

                         a scene supersedes
                                        I see my mother in a handmade cotton
dress

sorting through strawberries

                         I'm struck by her
   we went in the shallow of the forest
      to forage for lilies of the valley
                                the aromas of forest and perfume in my hair
our apartment filled with her

the plaintive boat ride on the pond
filled with large water lilies

      do I dare
    the scenes of you to unplay

                the brain to anchor to anything   at all
      the water lilies to harvest

the hair to unpin   the bed to unmake
      to make a stranger   of you

III

MOTEL ROOM 1

I draw the nylon-threaded curtains to a close.
I've been to a room not unlike this one once,
on a frenzied cross-country trip back to LA.

I was being driven. I was invaded
by dry sickly heat of either Utah or Arizona.
The desert held in its teeth, like a lizard

or a mountain mouse. Everything in this room
was a throwback, anachronistic.
A TV rested on a brown Formica dresser.

The green-on-brown carpet had a pattern
of stains & flowers. The bed, a queen
with more nylon. I fiddled with the drawer

of the nightstand. On my dominant side,
I withdrew it from itself. A copy of a Bible
slithered out. I opened it & whispered into the air.

There was nothing left to live for in the room.
Or outside it. The background was a culture
overthrown. There is a knock on the door.

ONE AFTERNOON IN AMSTERDAM

We watched a man making love to a woman in a manner
Of conventional intercourse on what could be called
A stage on a hot afternoon in Amsterdam breaths
Away from ours as we sat in what could be
Called the orchestra row the better seats in the room

I paid the scene a visit I was transfixed by the fluidity
Of their conventional nudity her aura was being
Moved from him to her like a ball at a game
Of tennis we were witnesses not voyeurs
To an exchange to what is called love on a sound

Stage set to our acts of love they were engaged in an act
Of mechanics but they weren't mechanical even though
Their familiarity said they did this on this stage with regularity
I won't ever know if they were students who needed
The money sex performers or a couple doing it to get

Off in bare feet they walked on the rectangular
Stage together holding each other's nude
Hands moving like artists models are
Used to moving in borrowed skin
Through a space occupied by people

Until comfortably settling into their nudity
In a folding chair before a group of art grad students
You did not show any signs of arousal your lips
Had a color of extinction your hand out of lock
With mine you were as dispassionate

As the folding chair you sat
In on the short walk back to our luxury
Hotel I wondered why you took me
To a peep show the heat &
Unclean sweat that formed & reformed

On my skin & yours was met by the cool inside-air inside
Our room the bed wasn't shaped like a square unlike
The stage the performers used for sex on it high thread-
Count sheets responded with a cool stiffness to the two
Bodies that fell & kept falling in and out of love

UNDERWATER

The naval admiral's shallow body
Is smaller than I imagined
Underwater
   In the nucleus of a nuclear submarine
Elusive to then Soviet fish spawning
On the sides of a metal ship

Adrift on driftwood
   Unmarked
Hardly belonging to any sovereign
 I am answering a question that keeps

Nagging at me

    Would I save him
  From a sniper,
     Rifle pointed
   At the center of a
      Life?

  If I am forced
Unnaturally to consider the matter

 Relying only on reflex

Unnaturally
If I am forced

The admiral's eyes mirror my transparency

As he wonders what I would do
If I am to choose

              Allegiances
          Redrawn or imagined
Why does it matter anyway?
     If placed in the unnatural
              Position

   I could become predator or savior
              If I am emptied
              Of the people I am

          Forced always to commit to love

HEATING UP

As you heat up in the sun

    Wet heat rising from the gills

        Nostrils flaring from a swim

In the torrents of the

                Ocean spilling you out along
        With frog-color algae

    Into a communal spill

           You glisten &

Spool into a concentric sphere

                Big enough to fit two

Ordinary people

        A pool that draws

        In with a gravitational

                Force bigger than

The undertow sucking in the sand

Under sunken foot

Your body in arrival

    Dumping itself into a multitude

Of just-arrived-to-the-shore

Smoothed rocks

       Letting out a sweaty idiom

  Between thigh & waist

The thrill rising & also falling

On the overheated bodies

Occupied in the sphere

LA EMPTY

I can count on my LA to empty
me out of dreams. The mind it burns
out, with its sunny sun.

That's lit up like a sun lamp,
on my face, casts a shadow
I cannot outrun.

The city's diminishing smog, lifts up
the horizon like collapsing vertebrae
and drives it into the ocean.

A COLONY

On a lukewarm August afternoon in Brooklin Maine,
I set out to a private beach on the Atlantic

Down saline-weathered steps. The summer house to my back,
Rising up out of the tall grass. The sand is more like glass than sand.

The multitude of exoskeletons, pulverized into a new species of sand.
I press my rubber-gloved feet into a decline of shore in the low tide.

Stepping down on a living colony of ocean animals. All by the dictates
Of evolution, dug in, inside their hard outer bodies. In ancient preparation

For an act not unlike this. I pick up one, of what I imagine is a member
Of a nuclear family, not unlike my own. A shell of typical size & unspectacular

Coloring. Of grey-on-white enamel. A raised texture to the touch,
As if set in Braille. As I ascend the stairs, back up to the house, I put my loot

Against my dominant ear. I am steeled to hear no song of a civilization
That predates mine, no soul traveling through time, no oracle to solve the eternal puzzle.

No dream about to break away. No scream. I don't dare imagine a single
Generation. The sirens put away their playthings. Odysseus long forgotten

& irrelevant. I don't imagine, any other hand that held up a shell
Like this one to the ear. The plainness of the shore to my back.

I hear the white murmur of the ocean through this historical artifact
& hear a voice that I recognize solely as my own.

NOT HAVING LEFT PARIS

I am forced awake to the scratching
Monotonous movements of a custodian
Sweeping up the street wet
From an overnight rain
The clean Rue du Mont Thabor
Made cleaner I've heard it before
As does Paris this Saturday morning
On a long-ago trip as I have made
My return my 1st-arrondissement pilgrimage
Absent of squalor rubs me awake

Lucidity is about to re-engage with the brain
And neutralize last night's fix of Ambien
Somehow hollowing out the brain
Cavity of brain overnight
The sleepers and I hear the roars of manual
Sweeps of a raw broom against a raw
Concrete from beds on restless streets
Of reticent arrondissements

The sunrise I missed rose like an egg
And remained a sunny-side-up
Yellow its shadow foreshadowed
By leave-taking to be undertaken
The idealism to be swept up
Into the Seine on the raw embankment

My Paris is about to drag on a Lucky
Strike pour into a pair of Levis
And keep awake in the coffee shop
Appointed with a preponderance of slick
Americana in its reticent arrondissement

The Paris I inhabit this morning is
Having to leave but not having left
The bakery where I will take communion
With an all-trip-desired croissant
Which I will enthrall in chunky strawberry
Jam and introduce to the mouth
In quick switchbacks will have eluded me

I set the crown of daisies on a bench in
The Jardin des Tuileries for a child having
Left the crown woven of white daisies
On a bench of Jardin des Tuileries was
Like throwing a grenade on continuous time

Leaving not yet but again the act
Of walking over a crack in the street
Looking back and it not being there

I have started to feel the pow pow
Of time of having left the street
With an exposed crack this time
Walking right over it

The museum exhibit emptied out
Of the mind like a penny out of a pocket
The thing of leaving before leaving
Staggering through time zones being
Stuck in a time zone somewhere between
Duty-free melancholy and nostalgia

Watching the moment of time take leave
Until another sun rises over Paris
I stand stripped to my skin before time

AT ONEGIN

The curtain rises, in a massive broom-
Sweep. A prelude to the composer's
Preamble, unrequited love is about to draw
Me out. Tatyana's love fever trickles out,

In perspiration beads. The soprano's
Makeup, setting up the face. In the letter-
To-Onegin aria. Outside her bedroom are
Sleepless birches guardian angels of the set

& auditorium. Love is about to lift me
Off my feet. Doomed, inside an opera,
Made from a novel set in verse.
Our girlish wishes —

Falling, into the arms of a prince.
Like the very first time at the Met.
Pushkin & Tchaikovsky, flanking
Me, I imagine, not the dozing off man.

Who can't help falling asleep to the beats,
Of unrequited love. In the parallel story line
Lensky's Arioso in Act 1, Scene 1, delivers:
Ya lyublyu vas!...

(I'm in love with you!...) Falling from
Formal vy, to the intimate *ty*,
In confession. Fated to loving Olga.
My daily betrayals. Catching a commuter

Train, to & fro life. The things that parting
Ways doesn't solve. As I see our distance
Grow, from the side-view mirror, computer
Bag, over-the-shoulder. Head, about to be

Held, in your lap. On the commuter train,
Succumbing to a prefabricated seat.
The Chagalls. Each in the entry points.
In the south, *The Triumph of Music,*

Red, unlike the faded velvet seat cushions
In the auditorium. *The Sources of Music,*
In the north, in yellow Technicolor
Backdrop, rehearse scenes of upside

Down people & angels, floating in music.
Of a girl who falls out of the sky.
She is unnoticed; that she is suffering.
When you became a woman unnoticed.

From that night, into the morning. Her
Waist, wider. Not vulnerable. The spine,
Less prone to yielding. As you became
Effortless, as yourself. The watchful

Woman. Eyes full of fullness. Words rising
To meet a breath. To recite a novel, set in
Verse. Performed on the wrong side of the
World. On a stage of the Met. The fan's

Tossed bouquet landing at her feet.
Sweeping up the stillness of the falling
Curtain. Opening to a full house, of the
Audience's gasps. In Act 2, Act 1, at dawn

The suffering Lensky, mourns his by-gone
youth in, *Kuda, Kuda, Kuda vy udalilis.*
As he begs the imaginary Olga to pay him a
Visit. Olga may never come. As he foresees,

His death, in the duel with Onegin. His
Suffering is unnoticed. As he falls. As I can,
Sometimes, fall. *Ах, Ольга, я тебя любил!*
(Oh, Olga, I was in love with you!)

Сердечный друг, желанный друг,
(My beloved, desired friend,)
приди, приди!
(come, come to me!)

Желанный друг, приди, я твой супруг,
(Oh much-coveted friend, come, I am your
eternal beloved), *приди, я твой супруг!*
(Come to me, I'm your eternal beloved!)

Приди, приди!(Come, come!)
Я жду тебя, желанный друг,
(I am here, waiting for you, my desired friend)
приди, приди, я твой супруг!

(Come, come, I am forever your beloved!)
Куда, куда, куда вы удалились,
(Where, where, oh where have you gone),
златые дни, златые дни моей весны?

(The happy, joyful days of my youth?)
As Tatyana leaves the stage, every night.
As if for the last time. As I leave the Met.
That night. As if for the last time.

THE PORTRAITIST

The genetics and muscle that is in me lay
expressed on her sedulously put
together canvas. So she said

at first. I was an infant in yellow infantilized.
On second, the ghost of our paternal
grandmother mocked me

on the canvas. The sitting began and ended
in fits and hard work
from sitter and portraitist.

My fits, my twitches are prominent.
I wore a constant scowl
and so did she.

Ours was an exchange between a little sister
and a bigger sister, in the American
dacha on long island.

Far from the Soviet dacha
but not close to a revelation. A second act
for me. A third for her.

The paint on paint continued to say
more about her than me. More of how
I am cemented in her.

We exchanged a time clock,
immortal. As if my flesh is her paint
and brush. And she will keep

me on this canvas. More than a sister.
And I stay her faithful
sitter.

A NOVEL NOT WRITTEN

Chapter 1

Her thoughts begin like all thoughts in brains of her species, at once adrift &
lumpy like the winter day getting under way one snowflake at a time. It's too
early for her, a person more in sync with the pattern of the night, the moon
always in place, with a beam more permanent than the sun's that gives itself
away day in & day out.

She is traveling with a man she loves now & yesterday & tomorrow. The night
before their trip she read him a Raymond Carver poem "A Poem Not Written." (where
water comes together with other water).

Love is dispensed in degrees of shared suffering;
        love's dissonance combines together with love's dissonance. The couple
on the balcony in Vienna is made immovable, in denial of time becoming
fire. He is in love with someone who is carved. Only her eyes tell him she's alive.
He will die with her one day of old age. Until then, he recites her the *Elements of the
Periodic Table*: 1. Argon, 2. Carbon, 3. Hydrogen, 4. Gold.

love
        from too much suffering, it stops being like other people's suffering; those who
are happy inside their own happiness, and those who are unhappy, unlike others.

Is love possible outside the skin of the novel, a poem, a business document?

freely,
        for love,
                for love that is learned by heart,
        for a house that is broken in,
        for a child who combines with another child,
                for the love that becomes part of one's charter.

UNREQUITED BY THE SUN

       I stare into the sun without protective eye gear,
Gearing up for high risk

       The doom taking me on a carpet ride   circling around loss's motion

       It receives me in a half-hush,
Like when you decided that love couldn't support air

       The sun is as bright as the sun,
Arriving at a close   an eye to shun the sun beneath a closing eyelid

       What if we feed spoonfuls of sugar to each other under the stare of the sun?
We would go to dig the fields, sowing our dreams for the next generation

       The deflating atlas filling up with sun rays
Children at play with decay,

       If silence had a sound, it would sound like loss without a heartbeat
A ghost moving in for good,

       Time, a strand in travel

CLOSER TO ROME

You taught me how to slay a chicken,
you would buy on the cheap from a
supermarket in the Roman port city of Ostia.
These weren't divided villas for the Roman

Condo experiment of the 1st Century.
We lived there in a shared breath with other
immigrants waiting to be admitted.
We waited. Collecting each other's tears

into the pages of unread books. To forget
the one who was left behind, waiting
for his own death sentence at trial.
More life to steal.

In elementary school, you could not stop
reading literature of high Romanticism.
In the dark blue of night. By a corded lamp,
inside a mahogany wardrobe, that took

up much of the hallway outside your
parent's bedroom; one of three rooms in
postwar Soviet communal dormitory.
With back leaning on a faded wall,

I trace you reading & listening to your
mother's footsteps approach;
putting an end to near-morning dreaming,
in your own goose-feather bed.

Under unforgiving stairs. Leading
out to another cold winter. Taking
me away, to my own footsteps,
in the snow, not yet fallen.

LOCKED (VIA AUXERRE FRANCE)

The cabin for four passengers trembles
As its weight bores into the track
A frozen-in window looks back

A pigeon in serenade settles
In between mason stones the walled
Courtyard fills up

With what sounds like a scream
Workers in the apartment across
The way with Eastern European accents

Plainly observed from a tall
Over-sized window built by Baron
Haussmann Napoleon III's city planner-célèbre

Begin to hammer & tighten
Screws they arrive like clockwork
Beginning & ending the day

Fulfilling a plan we are
Also visitors fulfilling a plan
Of our own as this courtyard

Records the sounds of restlessness
Coming & going a civilization
Lost & regained

In one snap of la minuterie
An automatic on & off switch
Lighting the way up

As vertigo unbalances underfoot
Ascending two steps at a time
Swept up in a summer draft

The overwhelming heat rising
To the 4th floor merging with air
Made in sleep

There was a full moon that rose
Too high my neck couldn't
Support the sight blocking

Curved planks the landlord expected
Us to shutter the windows before
Leaving the apartment trapping the thin

Symmetry of cool inside-air locking
the heat & whatever it brings out
Manmade artifacts in survival

Guarded by luck or maybe by something
Not man-made the rue traces
Back to war era steps

The train's weight roars
Into more summer to be had
Locking in this morning

THE APARTMENT ON RUSSIAN HILL

The floor-to-ceiling window peeled open a city
in disquiet, on the Pacific Rim. By day a tulip, by night
a monster. It hung over Russian Hill like a light bulb.
It accepted the visitors like an elevator car.

A large table in the dining room mapped out someone's
unhappy life, sitting in the wood. We drank & ate in the hill,
in the disquiet of hunger & thirst. We were framed, by love.
At night a bed branded us, in hieroglyphics.

We parsed the rings of unhappiness on our skins,
like animals in the wild. A lemon tree with large fruit
stood guard. Each morning, the apartment woke up
to primary colors, the sunlight beheld in the tulip.

You lay on the threshold, in conversation with monsters.
The tulip fell dark. The cable car on the hill punched
down the street with rehearsed confidence. It makes
a full stop for me.

I survey passengers engaged in modern life,
entangled in cords, listening to the passage of time.
As I fall, silent for now. Hopping off for now,
walking up the hill.

NOTES

"Ode to Strunk and White" is partly a cut-up. It is dedicated to my bother-in-law, Bill in whose family home in Brooklin Maine, the idea for the poem began. On leaving New York, E.B. White, the co-author of *Elements of Style*, settled in Brooklin, Maine, with his wife Katharine. Friends called him Andy.

"Locked (via Auxerre France):" The second part of the poem takes place on a train from Paris to Auxerre, the gateway to Chablis and the rest of Burgundy, which was the end destination that summer.

"Portrait of Bella:" Bella is my mother.

"Closer to Rome" is drawn from the second European city we settled in, for almost four months, on our way to the US from the former U.S.S.R.

"Amour Absolu," from the French, meaning unconditional love.

"The Apartment on Russian Hill:" The poem refers to a neighborhood in San Francisco.

The poem "A Colony" takes place in Brooklin, which is a small coastal town in Maine, an hour outside of Bar Harbor.

"Taking Down the New Year's Tree:" A Christmas tree in the former Soviet Union was referred to as a new year's tree.

"At Onegin:" The poem's name, comes from *Eugene Onegin*, a novel in verse written in the 19th Century by Aleksandr Pushkin, Russia's greatest poet. Tchaikovsky adapted the novel by the same name into a lyric opera. To reflect a modern outlook on romantic love, my translation of the libretto in places into English is deliberately not literal. I translated the word "супруг" which in Russian means husband or spouse as "beloved."

ACKNOWLEDGEMENTS

I am humbly grateful to the editors of the following publications in which these poems or versions of these poems first appeared:

Prelude "Out of the Frame"

Small Orange Journal "Closer to Rome"

The Indianapolis Review "One Afternoon in Amsterdam," and "The Apartment on Russian Hill"

Spillway "Monolith"

Cathexis Northwest Press "A Love Song"

Cleaver "Walking Through the Underworld"

Wild Roof Journal "Motel Room 1" and "The Long Drive"

Sunspot Literary Journal "Unrequited by the Sun"

Aji Magazine "Day's Break" and "Portrait of Bella"

Bangalore Review "In the Footsteps of Telemachus"

The Lake "Taking Down the New Year's Tree"

The Concrete Desert Review "In the Fish Tank" and "The Flow of Good & Evil"

Sleet "Together, Alone"

A Silent World in Her Vase "From LA with Love"

Red Fez "Amour Absolu"

Rabid Oak "Ode to Strunk and White"

Saccharine Poetry "Sunday Morning," Beach-Bound" and "Birth's Order"

The Write Launch "Locked (Via Auxerre France)," "Don't Tell the Women," and "Underwater"

Deep, enormous gratitude to Erica Wright, without whose close counsel, fine-tuned ear to poetic phonics, precision of language, and above all, skilled attention to lineation, this book wouldn't have come to fruition.

Kind thanks to the 92Y, specifically Ricardo Maldonado and Sophie Herron. Many thanks to Mark Wunderlich in whose class I re-engaged with form. To Nathalie Handal, an angel in form and spirit, who tirelessly asked me to quiet the noise and find my pulse.

Enormous gratitude to Kyle Dacuyan at The Poetry Project at St. Mark's Church, whose poems are breathtaking.

Gratitude to Alex Neceda, reference librarian at Larchmont Public Library for posting *After the Rain* on the library's Instagram and archiving it in the library's local history room.

Kindest thanks to Ralph Angel, who in the summer of 2017, told me to go home and make "an object of art," a collection of poems. I will always miss you.

Great gratitude goes to Carol Hayes who with great care supported me as the poems began to emerge.

Many thanks to Rimma, for reading every poem closely; to Julia for whom I recited early work and for her private recitals of Chopin and Beethoven when we were girls; to Marcia, who saved my earliest faxed poems and for always being a loyal reader; and to Vika, who read nascent poems as they emerged with so much love.

Gratitude: Carlie Hoffman for her friendship and help in finding a home for my poems, Gary Light for an everlasting friendship and translating poems into Russian for my mother, poets anonymous (Susan, Cynthia, Lori, Lily, Fanny and Damon), Ms. Harris (Finley's 4th-grade teacher who invited me to read my poems in his class), Marylin Cooperman for lifting the burden, Jill and Hilary for their love, Tom and Kathy who moved me to write *In the Footsteps of Telemachus*, gorgeous Karin, for your photographs of me and your design of stellahayespoet.com, dearest Jason, Bill Sky, one of my dearest friends on earth, Tanya whom I love, my loving mother and Volodya (for reading coaching), Jane (our hero), Laura, Peter, Susan, Andrew, beautiful Kushka and Alessa, and Bill whom we miss.

Thank you to Jed Steele for a trip to Steele in Lake County in fall of 2012 where I began to write poems again, after what seemed like the break of a lifetime. Quincy, thank you for encouraging me to see that there was no good reason why I shouldn't write again, if at the time, only for the heavenly bodies above.

I am deeply grateful to DeSales Harrison who persuaded me that this book mattered no matter what. Who urged me to listen to my Muse, and no other. And for the kindest appraisal of my book and work.

Gail Wronsky, my editor at What Press Books for believing in the book and for choosing *One Strange Country* for publication. Thank you to the collective which incudes, Karen Kevorkian, Chuck Rosenthal, Gronk, Elena Karina Byrne as well as everyone else in the group I have not named. And to Ash Good.

Deepest gratitude for EVERTHING to David St. John. You were my first teacher. You are so kind and loving.

And always to my mother, Alla, Dade, Margot & Finley — without whom nothing matters.

WHAT
BOOKS
PRESS

LOS ANGELES